Wow!
CHRISTMAS

To Chris and Sarah, for sparking the creative imagination in me;
to Chloe, for being my co-explorer in all our creative missions under
the dining room table; to Mitch, for always encouraging me to keep
my creative fire alight; and to the Ultimate Creator, thank you for the
creative blessings and inspiration you give me every day.

Text copyright © 2022 Martha Shrimpton
Illustrations by Sarah Nolloth
This edition copyright © 2022 Lion Hudson IP Limited

Published by
Candle Books
Part of the SPCK Group
Studio 101, The Record Hall, 16-16A Baldwins Gardens, EC1N 7RJ London, UK

ISBN 978 1 78128 424 7

First edition 2023

Acknowledgments
Designed by Karen Hood

A catalogue record for this book is available
from the British Library

Produced on paper from sustainable sources
Printed and bound in China, May 2023

Wow!

CHRISTMAS

Creatively explore stories in the Bible

MARTHA SHRIMPTON

ILLUSTRATED BY SARAH NOLLOTH

CANDLE BOOKS

The Wow! Series

Connect creatively with your maker, your family, and your community with this series of books exploring stories and themes found in the Bible.

Wow! Hello creative explorer! I am so glad that you have joined me on this mission to uncover the awesome story of Christmas! What an exciting journey there is ahead! So, grab the rest of your creative team (friends and family) because we are about to dive into these stories by playing, celebrating, and creating. Let's go!

Pray || Pause || Play || Create || Celebrate || Communicate

PRAY
Wow! Hello God... Opportunities to pray in a creative way, by yourself or with others.

PAUSE
Wow! Time to pause... Take some time out to reflect on a part of the story, and how it fits with your life now.

PLAY
Wow! What a show... Ideas to get you on your feet and having a bit of fun exploring the story.

CREATE
Wow! Let's create! Fun crafts and creations that help you to explore some of the story's themes.

CELEBRATE
Wow! That's cool! Rejoice and celebrate together as you discover things that amaze you about God in each story.

COMMUNICATE
Wow! Can we chat? A chance to chat and connect with each other, using parts of the story as conversation starters.

TOP TIP!
At the start of each chapter, you will spot a passage reference to find in your Bible. This will lead you to the story we will be exploring together! So, why not read the story in your Bible before you start your creative journey?

To find more creative resources, including storytelling videos of each story by Martha, and creative ways of exploring Bible stories with your family and community, visit the Nimbus Collective website at www.nimbuscollective.org

Nimbus Collective is an organization founded by Martha Shrimpton. It is aimed at helping you to connect in a creative way with yourself, your community, and God.

Contents

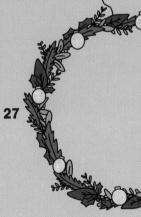

Flash! Sparkle! Shine!

Jesus brought light to the world

JOHN 1:1–18

BETHLEHEM

In the beginning everything was dark; there was nothing to see, until...

— FLASH! SPARKLE! SHINE! —

The world lit up as God showed us his creation and gave us his promise that he would always be with us!

Fast forward quite a few years, and a baby was born in a place called Bethlehem. It was said that this baby was going to be the "light of the world"! Not like a light bulb, or the sun and the moon, but a person who would bring love, peace, and joy.

This baby's name was Jesus. He was God's son. God sent him to the world so that we could have a friendship with him.

You see, when Jesus was born, he brought light to the world because his story gives everyone so much hope.

So, what about us? Why don't we bring some light to the people around us too? How can we do this? Time for some creative exploring!

Wow! What a story!

WANT TO READ MORE ABOUT LIGHT?
Why not dive into the story by reading **JOHN 1:1–18** in your Bible

OR you could start your creative adventure right away!

GLOW AND GO!

Wow! Did you know the longer and closer a glow-in-the-dark star is held under a light the *brighter* it glows?

This is like us and God. The longer we spend with God, the more we glow and reflect his light too. Not only that, but God also wants to spend time with us! How cool is that?

Let's get creative!

Why don't you try putting a glow-in-the-dark star under a lamp? As it sits there, ask God to help you to spend more time hanging out with him and to help you to reflect his light to other people.

Wow! Time to pause...

SMALL LIGHT
SHINE BRIGHT

Two thousand years ago, God made a light so bright that it could be seen from earth shining brighter than all the other stars! This was the sparkling star that led so many people to Jesus.

To everyone's surprise, this "light" came to the world as a tiny little baby! Later, Jesus would claim not only to bring light but to be the light in the world himself!

Have you ever lit a small tea light in a dark room? Did you notice how the light somehow spills into every tiny nook and corner?

Maybe our challenge for this festive season is to be the light too? We may feel small ourselves, but when we shine bright, it will brighten any room we enter!

Your "light" could be making someone laugh or smiling at a person as you walk past them. Perhaps it is giving a small encouragement to a friend by telling them how great you think they are? No matter how small your action, you will be surprised at how bright your light will shine.

Let's get creative!

Turn off ALL the artificial lights in a room and find a small candle to light..

Ask an adult to help you light the candle and fill the dark room with light.

Take a moment to think about how you could bring light into the world. Why not tell someone about what ideas you came up with?

NEWS FLASH!

Can you imagine what the people of Bethlehem thought when they saw a very bright star in the sky? It can't just have been the wise men who saw it! Who else saw the star? What do you think they thought it was? Why were people so excited about it?

Let's act!

It's time to create a scene to perform called "News Flash!" A scene is a way of telling a story by acting it out. You will play the role (the character) of a news presenter on live TV. Your "breaking news" will be about this very bright star in the sky!

YOU WILL NEED:

a costume to help you look like a news presenter
a prop to use as a microphone
  (a spoon or a hairbrush)

STEP 2

Create a script (the words) for your scene that you will say as the news presenter. Think about all the facts you want to include and use as much descriptive language as possible to help the audience picture the bright star.

At the beginning, make sure you introduce your story and yourself as your character. For example, you could say something like, "Hello and welcome to this breaking news report! My name is Louise Tiffin and here are the headlines for today..." Think about the emotions your character might be feeling and include these in your script. They could be really excited about this bright star, or perhaps they are scared!

STEP 1

Decide what you want your news presenter character to sound and move like. You may decide they are very flustered about having to present breaking news, or perhaps they are very calm and have a serious voice.

TOP TIP: When you create your character, try to change your tone of voice and your body language to make them look and sound different from you! This makes the character unique and fun to watch.

STEP 3

Once you have written your script, read it out loud as your character and rehearse your scene until you know your lines off by heart.

STEP 4

When you are ready, perform your brilliant scene for an audience!

Wow! Let's create!

HE HUNG THE STARS IN THE SKY

Isn't it cool how God used a bright star in the sky to point people to the exact place where Jesus had been born? Why not create your own little star garland to hang up in your home? On it, you can write down the names of all the people you would like to tell the story of Jesus' birth and the first Christmas to.

Let's get creative!

YOU WILL NEED:

ribbon
bright shiny paper
scissors
a pen
sticky tape

STEP 1 Draw ten star shapes on the back of your shiny paper. Remember every star is different, some big and some small. Don't feel like the stars need to be perfect!

STEP 2 Cut out all your star shapes.

STEP 3 Write a different name on each star for every person you would like to tell the story of Jesus to.

STEP 4 Cut your ribbon to about the length of 1 metre (3 ft).

STEP 5 Use the sticky tape to attach the back of the star onto the ribbon about 10cm (4 in) apart.

STEP 6 Hang up your garland where you will see it!

TOP TIP! To make your garland even more shiny and special, you could attach your stars to fairy lights to give them that extra little twinkle!

A FLASH OF INSPIRATION

It's awesome how light can create so many colours and shapes! The light source can be from the same place but can cause so many different reflections and effects when it hits different objects.

How about when the sun comes out after the rain and beautiful colours shine in the sky as a rainbow?

Or think about how the morning sunshine peaks its head over the horizon and the sky turns orange. Then at dusk, the sunshine says goodnight and the sky turns pink.

Amazing patterns even happen when light hits water, and it sparkles and glitters!

Let's get creative!

YOU WILL NEED:

a light source
   (e.g. a lamp or torch)
a bowl of water
a mirror
a glass jar or vase
see-through coloured plastic
   (if you have some available)

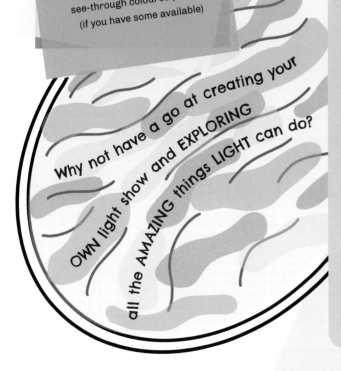

Why not have a go at creating your OWN light show and EXPLORING all the AMAZING things LIGHT can do?

STEP 1 Gather all the different objects you would like to use to help reflect the light. Set them up in an interesting pattern to create light reflections together.

STEP 2 Turn all artificial light sources off so your one light source will shine brightly onto your objects.

STEP 3 Turn on your light source and explore all the reflections and colours you can make when the light hits your objects. You could shine a lamp on a bowl of water and create ripples to see how the light dances. Or you could shine a torch onto a mirror and see how the light reflects off it into a different part of the room.

STEP 4 Choose a piece of music to play behind your light show and create your very own light performance!

STEP 5 Gather an audience and show them your fantastic light show!

Wow! Can we chat?

YOU'RE A STAR

There are some people we know who really make us smile. They encourage us or are there for us when we really need them.

Have you ever heard yourself say the words, "You're a star!" to a friend or a family member?

Think about who the "stars" are in your life – the people who have helped you or who make you smile. Who would you like to thank for lighting up your day?

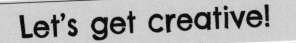

Let's get creative!

Why not have a chat with one of the people you've thought about, or send them a letter, to tell them how thankful you are for the light they bring to your life?

Write their name or draw a picture of them in the spark shapes here to help you remember who they are.

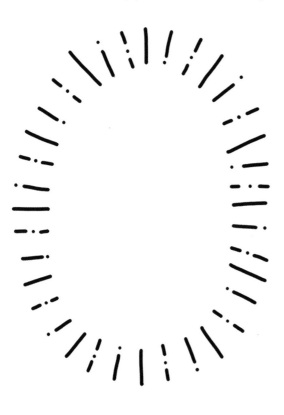

Extraordinary, Not Ordinary!

The ordinary people who discovered something amazing

LUKE 2:8–20

The day was turning to dusk and a few shepherds were gathered around a campfire keeping warm while they watched their sheep. This evening was nothing out of the ordinary. Each night, the men would sit in the same place, at the same time, doing the same thing. But all that was about to change...

Something extraordinary happened and the humdrum of their day-to-day lives was shaken up big time!

Suddenly, a bright light shone into the shepherds' eyes and blinded them for a moment. As their eyes drew back into focus again, they saw an angel standing before them! The unbelievable thing was that this angel had been sent from God to give them a message. These shepherds, who thought of themselves as the most ordinary people around, were being sent the most extraordinary message there ever was!

The angel spoke to the shepherds and said, "I bring you good news that will bring great joy to many people! Today in Bethlehem a saviour has been born to you. He is the son of God, the Lord! This is a message for you: you will find a baby wrapped in cloths and lying in a manger."

The shepherds couldn't believe that out of all the people in the world, they had been chosen to receive this message.

Well, this one was a no-brainer! They had to go and meet this remarkable baby, the saviour of the world.

The shepherds left in a hurry and began the most amazing adventure to meet the baby Jesus!

Wow! What a story!

WANT TO READ MORE ABOUT THESE AWESOME SHEPHERDS?
Why not dive into the story by reading it in your Bible in
LUKE 2:8–20?

OR you could start your creative adventure right away!

Wow! Hello God...

THE SHEPHERDS
RENAMED

The shepherds thought they were ordinary. Lots of people told them they were ordinary! They had very ordinary lives and a very ordinary job! However, God sent his angel to them and showed them that they were extraordinary. They deserved to hear this amazing news first, before anyone else!

God renamed the shepherds as worthy and exceptional, even when they didn't believe that themselves.

God thinks you are extraordinary and worthy of knowing this story too!

Take some time to talk to God and ask him to help you to know what he thinks of you too. He thinks you are extraordinary. He thinks you are precious. He loves you!

Let's get creative!

Fill in the picture below with your name. Underneath, complete the words, "I am extraordinary" to be reminded of the fact that God thinks you are amazing.

Hello, my name is ....

I am ....

I CAN TELL BY YOUR FACE

The shepherds must have gone through so many different emotions when they met the angel, started their journey, and met Jesus!

They were so full of excitement that they couldn't help but share the news with everyone they met. But there were probably times when they also felt a little scared and confused, and lots of other emotions too!

Let's get creative!

Have a look at the words above each blank face below. How do you think the shepherds were feeling at each stage in the story?

On the blank faces, draw the expressions showing each emotion the shepherds may have felt. Have you ever felt emotions like this yourself?

The shepherds...

watching the sheep...

The shepherds felt

....

meeting the angel...

The shepherds felt

....

hurrying to Bethlehem...

The shepherds felt

....

meeting the baby Jesus...

The shepherds felt

....

telling everyone about what they had seen...

The shepherds felt

....

Wow! What a show...

AN EXTRAORDINARY MISSION!

The angel Gabriel has been given a special mission by Heaven Headquarters (HQ). His mission is to tell a small group of shepherds, who are sitting on a hillside in the late evening, all about the exciting news of what is happening in Bethlehem and how they must go and see Jesus!

Heaven HQ has told Gabe that he needs to communicate the news in the most exciting and exhilarating way possible. He can even use the heavenly gospel choir for his mission message if he wants to!

Let's act!

It's time to create your own mission message! You will play the role of Gabe, who is giving a Heaven HQ message to the shepherds.

STEP 1 Decide how you want Gabriel to stand and sound. Maybe you have decided that he will move with skipping movements, as if he is flying, and has a high-sounding voice. Or perhaps you want him to walk with a stomping motion because he has never stood on earth before! Perhaps he has a low, loud voice that booms across the hillside!

STEP 2 Once you have created your character, decide on what Gabriel will say in his mission message. What are the most important parts of the story that you want to include? Maybe it's important that he tells the shepherds about Jesus being born in Bethlehem, that he will bring peace to all people, and that he is there to give good news to all people?

STEP 3 Create a script with all the important information you have gathered from the story. Your mission message needs:

- A good opening; it could be something like,

  "I am Gabriel from Heaven HQ! Your mission, if you choose to accept it…"

- A middle with all the information you would like to include in a playful and fun way. Maybe you could pretend to get the message wrong, or the angels' singing could be out of tune!
- A strong ending that tells the shepherds to start their journey to find the baby Jesus.

STEP 4 Rehearse your mission message in character until you feel confident. Gather some people to make an audience and perform your fantastic mission message!

AND THEY DIDN'T STOP TALKING!

When the shepherds met Jesus, they were so overwhelmed by what they had experienced that they couldn't help but tell everyone about their story.

Can you imagine the shepherds hanging out with their friends and repeating the awesome story to anyone who would listen?

What do you think people would have remembered from their story? The peace the shepherds felt? The awesome heavenly choir of angels? The ordinary shepherds meeting the most extraordinary baby ever?

Let's get creative!

Why not create your own newspaper called *The Bethlehem Bulletin* and write a front-page article all about what the shepherds were talking about?

Once you've written it, you could make multiple copies and give them to your friends to spread the story, just like the shepherds!

THE BETHLEHEM BULLETIN

SUPER SANDAL SALE!

CENSUS CHAOS: all accommodation in Bethlehem fully booked

I AM **EXTRAORDINARY**

Did you know that this extraordinary story is for ordinary people like us because God believes that we are extraordinary too? Just like the shepherds!

God designed us. He made us different from each other, and unique. When Jesus grew up, he showed everyone just how much he loved and treasured each person individually!

So, what makes you extraordinary? What are the things that make you different from other people? Is it the things you like doing, or how you are good at caring for other people? Or maybe it's how you make people laugh, or a particular skill you have?

Let's get creative!

In the gallery frames below, draw pictures to celebrate what makes you extraordinary!

Something that I enjoy doing

Something that I am skilled in

An extraordinary part of my personality

THE MARSHMALLOW STORIES

What do you think the shepherds got up to on those late nights when they were sat together on the hills watching the sheep?

Maybe they were all gathered around a big fire sharing stories while toasting marshmallows?

Why not create your own version of the shepherds sharing stories and marshmallows?

Let's get creative!

Gather some friends and pretend that you are gathered around an open fire late at night while drinking hot chocolate and toasting marshmallows. (If you are with an adult, you could do this around a real fire one evening!)

Sitting in a circle, take it in turns to tell the story of the first Christmas together. However, instead of one person telling the whole story, say one sentence each. Each sentence should tell the next part of the story until you have told the whole story together as a group!

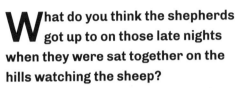

TOP TIP:
If you find telling the story in this way too easy, you can make it a little harder by each person saying just one word at a time. Not only do you have to form the story together as a group, but you must also form sentences together too!

Are We There Yet?

The wise men who journeyed for miles

MATTHEW 2:1–18

A long time before Jesus was born, some wise men had dedicated their lives to studying all the stars in the sky. They knew every part of the night sky like the back of their hands, so you can imagine their reaction when they noticed something very odd.

"An intergalactic irregularity in the deep night sky!" one declared! (To you and me, that means a big, bright star that has never been seen!)

They knew this star meant that a new king had been born and that it would lead them exactly to where the baby might be. Something amazing had happened!

So, what did the wise men decide to do? They packed their bags and set out, travelling for nights on end as they followed this big star with the brightest shine. This really would be the journey of a lifetime for them!

Wow! What a story! What a miracle!

WANT TO READ MORE ABOUT THESE WISE MEN?
Why not dive into the story by reading it in your Bible in **MATTHEW 2:1–18?**

OR you could start your creative adventure right away!

TOP-SECRET STEPS

Years ago, a group of walkers began to leave little messages to each other in secret places on their hiking routes. They left notes and other surprises like energy bars in tins for others to find.

Roll on a few years, and this treasure hunt is still going on. It's now called "geocaching" and has turned into a worldwide game of hide and seek with these mystery packages! Every time someone uncovers a mystery box, it brings a lot of excitement and eagerness to open it quickly to find out what's inside!

How cool would it be to leave secret prayers around for people to find as they walked too?

It could be a prayer thanking God for how amazing he is, written on a little stone for someone to stumble upon. Or a prayer praising God for his beautiful creation, written on a scrap of paper and tied to a tree branch for someone to read and experience God's blessing too!

Let's get creative!

Why don't you create top-secret prayers and hide them for people to discover?

YOU WILL NEED:

scrap paper, small stones,
    or scrap material
colourful pens

With a brightly coloured pen and scrap of material, a stone, or piece of paper, write down a prayer thanking God for his beautiful creation. Hide it in your local park for someone to find (being careful that your note does not turn into litter)!

Wow! Time to pause...

A NEW PATH

Wow! So many people we meet in the Christmas story didn't know how the story would end. The wise men were following the star not knowing where it would lead. The shepherds were not sure what they would discover in Bethlehem when they eventually found baby Jesus, the Messiah. And Mary and Joseph didn't fully understand what it was going to be like being parents as Jesus grew up!

Sometimes not knowing where we are going can be scary! It can also feel exciting! Discovering something new – a different place or a new secret path – or meeting new people can be one of the best things we experience! You never know what you will find!

Later today, or as soon as you can, go for a walk in an area you know really well. Ask an adult to go with you.

Dare to take a path you've never been on before and see what exciting things you discover! You never know – you may uncover something wonderful!

TOO MUCH STUFF!

Do you ever struggle with knowing what to pack when you go on holiday? Will you need warm clothes or cool clothes? How many books should you take? How many pairs of shoes should you pack?

How do you think the wise men found packing for their long journey?

Do you think they knew what they would need or how long they could be gone for? Perhaps they ended up taking loads of luggage! Then the story finishes with an uplifting ending as the disciples can't help but worship Jesus!

Let's act!

It's time to create your own comedy mini-play!

A play is when people pretend to be different characters and act out a story together.

A comedy is a play where the words and actions make people laugh.

In this mini-play, called *Long Road Ahead*, the wise men are packing their bags with all sorts of funny things they think they will "need" for their journey following the star!

STEP 2

Create your script (the words you will say) by deciding on what items you will pack, and what emotions your character is feeling about packing and going on the journey.

TOP TIP: You can write down the words you want your character to say, or you could make them up as you go along. Either way, make sure you have a clear beginning, middle, and end to your play.

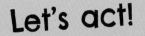

STEP 3

Practise your scene until you are confident in what you are saying and doing in your mini-play.

STEP 1

Create your wise man character. How can you change the way your voice sounds and the way you move?

TOP TIP: When performing comedy, the bigger your face expressions, the better! It will really make people laugh!

STEP 4

When you are ready, perform your mini-play to an audience!

Wow! Let's create!

MY MAP

When we go on a big journey, we often take a map with us. It might be a road map to show us which roads to drive on, or a map of the countryside showing us which paths to walk along. Or perhaps we have a map on a phone to reroute our journey if we get a little lost!

One thing we do not have is a map for our lives! A map to show us where we have come from and where we are going.

The awesome thing is that God is on the journey of our lives with us, and he knows the path we are on and where we are going! So, we don't need to worry! How cool is that?

Let's get creative!

Make your own "Life Map" showing where you have come from and where you would like to go.

YOU WILL NEED:

a big piece of paper
colouring pencils and pens to make
   your map extra bright

STEP 1 Draw a path or a road on your piece of paper. The start of the road represents when you were born, and the end of the road represents now, or even the future if you would like to think about that!

STEP 2 On the road you have created, draw pictures of the people you have met along the way, the things you've done that you're proud about, and the best places that you have visited or in which you have lived.

STEP 3 On the side of the road, draw pictures of the times you know God has been with you to help you. It could be a time when you were nervous or scared and God gave you peace! Or it could be a really happy memory of a time when you felt God's joy.

STEP 4 When you have finished drawing your pictures, colour in the road and shapes in bright colours. Take a step back from your picture and look at the path you have been on!

WOW! What a journey!

FOLLOW MY TRACK

The wise men had to track the path of the star to show them which direction to take on their journey. They had no map, only a star pointing the way!

Let's get creative!

Create a secret path for a friend to track!

STEP 1 Go for a walk in your local area. You may need to ask an adult to go with you. As you walk, leave arrow shapes on the ground made from sticks or leaves that you find on your way. You could also use some chalk to draw arrows that would wash away in the rain. Make sure the arrows are pointing in the direction of the route you want people to take.

STEP 2 When you have finished laying down your path, tell a friend that you have set out a journey for them and an adult to go on. They will know which direction to take by finding the arrows you have created.

STEP 3 Your friend can tell you if they were able to follow the path you have made. Then they can create a route for you to follow too!

WHAT DO YOU NEED TO PACK?

God has an amazing plan for you in your life! It even says so in the Bible. In Jeremiah 29:11, it says, "For I know the plans I have for you, plans to prosper you and not harm you, to give you hope and a future."

The path that God has laid out for you is thrilling and exciting, but he doesn't make you do it alone! He promises that he will give you all the things you need for your journey.

God can give you courage, wisdom, joy, patience, and even more. All you need to do is ask him!

Let's get creative!

What might you need God to give you for the life journey you are on? Talk with an adult about what those things could be.

In the suitcases here, write something down, or draw a picture to represent the gifts you are asking God to give you on your epic journey with him!

Love From Me. X

Christmas brings so many gifts to us all!

MATTHEW 2:9–12

The gift wrapped in golden paper and tied up with a big red bow sparkles as it sits neatly under the tree. It's been there for over a week, inviting people to shake it and squeeze it to work out what's inside, but still nobody can guess.

The label reads simply: "Love From Me" with a kiss.

Excitement bubbles as Christmas Day fast approaches. Then the wrapping paper will be eagerly torn off to reveal the most wonderful gift. Giving and receiving presents at Christmas brings so much joy, especially with gifts that are well received!

In the Christmas story, there are so many gifts given and received.

The gift of being pregnant given from God to Mary.

The gifts of gold, frankincense, and myrrh given to Jesus from the wise men.

And probably the biggest gift of all – God's gift to the world, his son, Jesus!

WANT TO READ MORE ABOUT THE WISE MEN'S GIFTS?
Why not dive into the story by reading it in your Bible in **MATTHEW 2:9–12**

Wow! What a story!

OR Or you could start your creative adventure right away!

Wow! Hello God...

THE PERFECT PRESENT

At Christmas, we have a lovely tradition of giving and receiving gifts. It is always very exciting when you have bought or made a present for someone that you know they will really love!

Wrapping the perfect gift and writing a name tag for the recipient to find the parcel under the tree is something that fills us with such joy! Especially when the gift has been hand-picked just for them!

At that first Christmas, God gave the world the gift of his son, Jesus. This was the most incredible present that he could have given because it would mean that we could have our own friendship with him!

In our lives, God blesses us with so many gifts that show us how much he loves us: our friendships, our homes, the food we eat... The list goes on!

Let's get creative!

In the presents below, draw or write down the gifts that God has given you in your life. As you draw your pictures, chat with God and thank him for the things he has blessed you with.

PEACE

When Jesus was born, a group of angels appeared in the sky and proclaimed amazing words! The lyrics of this epic hit were, "Glory to God in the highest, and peace to all the people he approves"! They are awesome words saying that God will give peace to his people.

Sometimes, life can feel very uncertain and scary, but the amazing thing is that God promises he will always give us peace!

Have you had a time in your life where you needed to know God's peace? Or perhaps there is something going on in your life right now?

Why not ask God to show you his peace now?

Let's get creative!

YOU WILL NEED:

a candle or fairy lights
some time to pause

STEP 1 Find a space that is quiet with no distractions.

STEP 2 As you think of the thing for which you need God's peace, light a candle or turn on some fairy lights. You may need an adult to help you with this.

STEP 3 Watch the light flicker and take a moment to pause.

STEP 4 Ask God to bring his gift of peace to you in the moments when you feel uncertain or scared.

▶ *Wow!* What a show...

IT'S A **GIFT!**

When everyone went to visit Jesus on that first Christmas, they brought him gifts. The wise men brought the baby gifts of gold, frankincense, and myrrh. They were very odd gifts to give a baby, that's for sure!

Do you think the shepherds gave Jesus one of their sheep as a gift?

Let's act!

Why not create your own comedy scene called "It's a Gift!" In the scene, each character gives Jesus a gift, but it turns out they have all given him the wrong one! It could be that they mixed up his present with a gift for their grandma, or they brought their shopping bag instead of the bag containing the presents for the newborn baby!

STEP 1 Decide which role you would like to play in your scene. It could be one of the wise men, a shepherd, or even a member of Joseph's family! If you have several people creating your scene, make sure you all have your own character to play.

STEP 2 Decide on the "wrong" gift that your character is going to give the baby Jesus. It could be something that you would usually give to a baby like a cuddly toy, or it could be something a little more unusual! Decide what you think will be funniest for your scene.

STEP 3 Create a structure for the scene. At the beginning, you will give your present. In the middle, once Mary has opened the gift, you need to explain what it is and why it is a good gift. At the end, you can decide if your character gives Jesus the present or if the present is taken back.

STEP 4 Write a script for your scene. If there is only one of you, this would be a "monologue", where one character speaks for the whole time. If there are two or more of you, maybe one of you can play the role of Mary or Joseph to have a two-way conversation.

STEP 5 Rehearse your comedy scene until it is ready, find an audience, and perform your fantastic play!

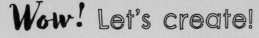

A CHRISTMAS **WREATH**

Christmas is a wonderful time to bless other people by giving them a special gift!

Why not make your own Christmas wreath to give to a friend as a present to decorate their house or to hang on their door?

Let's get creative!

YOU WILL NEED:

a bag to collect foliage
foliage, such as holly, fern leaves, and mistletoe

a wire coat hanger
some string and ribbon
a roll of tape
Coloured tags

STEP 1 With an adult, go outside with a bag and some secateurs to collect foliage to create your wreath. Make sure you only gather from places that you have permission to do so.

TOP TIP! Plants like fern leaves, mistletoe, and holly work a treat as they are very festive! However, beware that mistletoe is poisonous, so keep it well away from little brothers and sisters.

STEP 2 Bend your wire coat hanger into a circle shape, leaving the hook on the top.

STEP 3 Using your string, ribbon, and tape, begin to attach your foliage to the coat hanger. The fuller you can arrange the leaves, the better your wreath will look. Do this until the whole circle of wire is covered.

TOP TIP! To make your wreath even more colourful and festive, you could also tie some tinsel and baubles to the wire circle. This will bring a nice bit of sparkle to your wreath when the light catches it.

STEP 4 On a colourful paper tag, write a kind message to a friend to tell them how special they are. Leave the wreath on their doorstep as a lovely festive surprise!

Wow! That's cool!

A STORY OF MANY LAYERS

The first Christmas story is full of so many surprises. There are lots of exciting journeys, and twists and turns!

To celebrate such an epic story with so many parts to it, why not create a "Christmas pass the parcel" to play with your friends and to tell them about the series of events?

Let's get creative!

YOU WILL NEED:

lots of pieces of coloured card and pens
wrapping paper
two bags of chocolate coins (or other treats)

STEP 1

Write down the story of the first Christmas, divided into sentences with bullet points. You could divide the story into big chunks where you meet each character in the story. Or you could separate the story into smaller sections where you break down the story into events and even add in little sections of dialogue.

STEP 4

Lay the end story card on top of this little package along with one chocolate coin from the second bag. Then wrap this up with another layer of paper. Repeat this step until all the cards are gone and there is a treat, such as a chocolate coin, in every layer.

TOP TIP: Make sure the cards are wrapped up in the correct order, so that the outside layer has the start of the story.

STEP 2

Once you have split up the story, write each part onto its own individual coloured piece of card. Label your cards so you remember which order they go in.

TOP TIP: Why not decorate the cards with pictures or stickers and glitter to make them look extra cool?

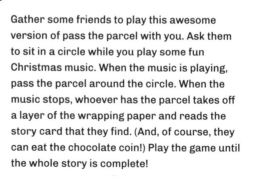

STEP 5

Gather some friends to play this awesome version of pass the parcel with you. Ask them to sit in a circle while you play some fun Christmas music. When the music is playing, pass the parcel around the circle. When the music stops, whoever has the parcel takes off a layer of the wrapping paper and reads the story card that they find. (And, of course, they can eat the chocolate coin!) Play the game until the whole story is complete!

STEP 3

Wrap up one of the bags of chocolate coins to go into the centre of your parcel.

FROM **HIM**

God gave Jesus to the world as a gift. He knew that Jesus could help the world by showing them love and miracles, teaching them all about how amazing God is, and leading them to have their own personal friendship with God too.

Let's get creative!

As you colour in this picture, why not talk to an adult about why you think God sent Jesus as a gift to the world?

"Whatever is good and perfect is a gift coming down to us from God…"
JAMES 1:17

Wait a Moment!

The excitement in waiting for Christmas to arrive

ISAIAH 7:14

Mary was pregnant for nine months, faithfully waiting for her baby to be ready to be born.

The wise men were patiently waiting for the stars to come out again, as it turned to night, so that they could follow the brightest star of all.

People had been desperately waiting for God to send a saviour for hundreds of years.

God had promised it in scriptures written in the Old Testament, the first part of the Bible.

In Advent, the four weeks leading up to Christmas Day, we enthusiastically wait for Christmas Day to arrive as the countdown begins.

We excitedly wait on Christmas Eve for when it is time to go to bed before the big day!

We often find ourselves waiting for Jesus to arrive too. We wait for him to shine his light into our lives, showing love, hope, and peace to us.

There is so much waiting in the Christmas story that we can explore... so go on! What are you waiting for? It's time for your creative adventure!

Wow! Waiting is a really hard thing to do but there is so much waiting in the Christmas story!

WANT TO READ MORE?
Why not dive into your Bible to read **ISAIAH 7:14** where the birth of Jesus is spoken about a long time before it happened?

OR you could start your creative adventure right away!

HOT CHOCOLATE PRAYER

Sometimes in life, we can find ourselves rushing around to get to the next place quickly. It might be to get a task done, to arrive at school or work, or because we just have so much to do that we are rushing to tick everything off our list!

However, God never rushes! Do you ever feel like you want something to happen in your life right away, like moving to a new house or wanting to do something you're not ready for yet?

In those moments, God will wait until the time is right, but he doesn't leave us when we are waiting. He is always there with us!

Let's get creative!

Take some time out for you and God. Talk to him about a time when you always find yourself rushing. It could be to rush to get out of the door or to get your homework done. Use this creative prayer to ask God to help you to slow down and to be present in every moment in your day, so you can remember he is with you.

Make yourself your favourite hot drink; it could be a hot chocolate or maybe tea!

As you wait for the hot water or hot milk to boil, talk with God. Ask him to help you to be patient when you are waiting for things to happen in your life.

As you hold your warm mug and wait for your drink to cool, talk with God. Ask him to be with you in the times that you are waiting for something to change in your life.

As you take your first sip, thank God for those moments when he blesses us with things we have been waiting for.

Wow! Time to pause...

I AM WAITING

In the Christmas story, so many people are waiting for something. Mary and Joseph wait for nine months for Jesus to arrive while Mary is pregnant, and the wise men wait for the stars to align in the sky to be able to follow the right one!

We often find ourselves waiting
for something in our own lives...
Waiting for a message
Waiting for a bus
Waiting for a cake to finish baking
Waiting for a friend to visit

Is there anything you are waiting for now? How do you feel when you are waiting for something?
Do you ever ask God to help you in the waiting? You could ask him to help you be more patient or to bring you peace while you are waiting.

Let's get creative!

Create your own "Waiting Poem Prayer" to God about when you are waiting.

Use the lines below as a starting point for your poem prayer. Once you've finished writing it, read it out loud as a prayer to God to help you in the times you are waiting for something.

When I am waiting for

....

help me to

....

When I am waiting for

....

help me to

....

When I am waiting for

....

help me to

....

When I am waiting,
God please be with me.

IT WAS TOLD BEFORE

Did you know that many years before Jesus was even born people were told that he was coming? However, nobody knew when or how, so when Jesus was born as a baby it was a total surprise to everyone!

In the Old Testament in the Bible, there were many prophecies given, which are messages from God about the future. These said that God would send someone to save the world and to help people to have their own friendship with God.

People couldn't believe it when they realized Jesus was the answer to all these prophecies from years ago! God kept his promises to all of us!

Let's act!

Create a scene to perform about these prophecies. For your scene, use the passage from Isaiah that we are exploring together: "Therefore the Lord himself will give you a sign: The virgin will conceive and give birth to a son, and will call him Immanuel." (Isaiah 7:14)

In the scene, a historian (someone who knows a lot about history), is on breakfast TV telling everyone about how all these predictions from the past have now come true. The historian character is really amazed and is struggling to believe it!

STEP 1 Create the historian character by thinking about how their voice sounds and how they walk.

TOP TIP! When you are acting as a character, it is great to change your voice and expressions to make the character look and sound different from you. You may even want to find a costume to wear.

STEP 2 Decide on three facts that the historian will give when they are being interviewed. You could use the quote from Isaiah about Jesus, or you could give facts about the events that happened when Jesus was born.

STEP 3 Create a script for your scene. Include your three facts and add in lines to show how the historian feels about all this coming true. Maybe they are extremely excited because they have been studying the prophesies for years, or maybe they don't believe that this baby is linked with the prophesies at all!

TOP TIP! To make it sound like an interview on breakfast TV, you could start your scene by saying good morning to the presenters. If there is someone else to act with you, they could play the role of presenter and ask you questions as you share your facts.

STEP 4 Rehearse your scene. When you are ready, show people your fantastic performance!

✂ Wow! Let's create!

COUNTING DOWN

At Christmas time, we celebrate Advent. This is the month we spend preparing and waiting for the celebration of Jesus' birth!

In the hustle and bustle of the Christmas festivities, Advent is a really great time to be able to remind ourselves of the true meaning of Christmas.

Let's get creative!

Why not make your own Advent calendar? This will remind you of the story of the first Christmas in the run up to 25 December.

YOU WILL NEED:

a Bible
two pieces of card
coloured pens and pencils
a glue stick
scissors

STEP 1 On one sheet of card, draw a picture that you want to appear on the front of your Advent calendar. It can be of anything you want. Make sure it fills the page and is as bright and colourful as possible!

TOP TIP! You could use glitter and stickers on your picture if you want to add an extra bit of sparkle!

STEP 2 With a pencil, lightly draw twenty-four squares on your picture and add a number from one to twenty-four to each square.

STEP 3 With an adult's help, use your scissors to cut around three sides of each of your squares so they can open like a window. Make sure you don't accidently cut all four sides as your window will fall off!

STEP 4 Apply glue to the back of your picture in places where there isn't a window flap. Stick your second sheet of paper directly behind your picture.

STEP 5 In the space behind each window, draw a picture from part of the Christmas story. For example, the star, a shepherd, or a gift from the wise men. OR you could use this as a calendar to help you pray. Behind each window, you could draw a picture of someone you want to pray for, meaning that you will pray for twenty-four different people over the whole of Advent!

WAIT AND SEE

The countdown to Christmas Day is so exciting! Especially on Christmas Eve, when there are only a few hours to go!

Why not make the waiting on Christmas Eve even more special and create your own "Wait and See" surprise? This is when you do a fun task in preparation for something happening the following day.
It could be...

- Arranging all the presents in a fun pattern or in order of who they are for.

- Laying the breakfast table with beautiful decorations, ready for everyone to enjoy on Christmas morning.
- Writing special name cards for people using pens, stencils or stickers, to help them find their seats when they are ready to sit down for Christmas dinner.

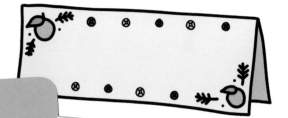

Let's get creative!

These are a few creative ideas, but you may have your own idea of a "Wait and See" surprise.

Write and plan your "Wait and See" surprise in the space so you are extra prepared when it comes to creating it on Christmas Eve!

I'm Planning a "WAIT AND SEE" Surprise

Wow! Can we chat?

JOY IN THE WAITING

Jesus looked just like any other baby. His mother, Mary, still had to change his nappies, feed him, and stop him crying! She watched him grow up into a boy, and a teenager, and then into a man!

Everyone had to wait for a long time until Jesus started to perform miracles and travel around teaching about God. They had to wait thirty years to be precise, because Jesus was about thirty years old when he started doing these things!

However, Mary found great joy in watching Jesus grow up. Most parents enjoy watching their children grow and creating a store of memories!

Let's get creative!

Ask your parent or guardian, or another adult, what it's been like watching you grow up. What is there about you that they treasure? It could be something funny you do or did, or a memory they share with you.

Or perhaps you want to think about yourself and a good memory you have of growing up?

In the picture frame above, draw a picture of the memory or the nice thing about you that you can treasure forever!

It's a Celebration!

Christmas is something to celebrate!

LUKE 2:1–20

Everyone was buzzing with excitement! Word was spreading fast around the town that Jesus had been born. It was rumoured that this was the baby they had all been waiting for! This baby was sent from God to be the saviour of the world!

Two thousand years later, this celebration is still going on – and the party will go on for centuries to come!

You see, Jesus being born completely turned history on its head.

That's because this monumental event now means that we can have a friendship with God!

So, let's hang up our tinsel and string up our lights! Let's sing louder than ever, share jokes, and laugh until late into the night!

If Jesus, sent from God to save the world, isn't a cause for celebration, then what is?

Wow! This really is a cause for celebration!

WANT TO READ MORE ABOUT JESUS' FIRST BIRTHDAY?
Why not dive into the story by reading it in your Bible in
LUKE 2:1–20?

OR you could start your creative adventure right away!

EVERYONE WELCOME

The best thing about the story of the first Christmas is that this tiny baby, Jesus, was going to grow up into a man who would do amazing things!

We know that Jesus was the son of God, and God sent Jesus to earth so that we could have our own relationship with him. Even today, we can just chat with God whenever we want! That is pretty cool.

The thing that is most cool, though, is that everyone is invited to have a friendship with God. Everyone is invited to celebrate the birth of Jesus together!

Let's get creative!

Next to each person in the picture below, write the name of one of your friends.

Pray that they will get to have a relationship with God too and feel joy this festive season! While you are praying, you could add to the picture of the party scene as a symbol of this joy.

Once you've done this, why not tell your friends you've been praying for them? Use this chance to tell them the amazing story of Christmas.

HEAVENLY HARMONY

When Jesus was born, even the angels celebrated by proclaiming praise to God. Imagine if instead of saying the words of praise, they had sung them?

The singing would have sounded like the most beautiful music imaginable – a phenomenal choir in the sky! This remarkable sight on a dark evening would have lit up the sky with celebration and glorious sound.

Music can often be something that stirs our hearts and souls. It makes us feel lots of different emotions. What emotions do you think the shepherds felt on that night when they heard the angels?

Let's get creative!

It's time to stop and imagine that scene now!

Turn all the lights off apart from any fairy lights you may have. Keep them switched on to help you imagine the starry night sky.

Find a piece of choral music that makes you feel wonder. The carol "O Holy Night" is always a beautiful piece of music around Christmas time.

While the music plays, sit or lie imagining... the beautiful heavenly harmony on that still night.

Wow! What a show...

CHATTER
AT THE INN

Bethlehem was rammed full of people all needing a room in which to stay. This was because of the census that was happening, which counted how many people were in the country.

Little did all the people in Bethlehem know that they were in a place that would go down in history! It was late at night, and across the town, the sound of a newborn baby could be heard...

This baby was Jesus! The baby who was going to grow up to be the saviour of the world!

The word spread like fire through Bethlehem. Everyone began to gossip about the news that the Messiah had been born and they were close to the action!

Well I never!

Let's act!

Create a short scene showing all the guests spreading the news about Jesus being born in Bethlehem. The scene is called "The Gossip in the Town".

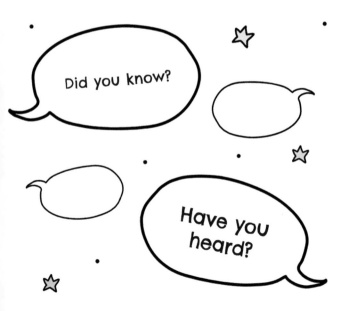

Did you know?

Have you heard?

STEP 1 Create as many different characters as you like by changing your tone of voice (the way your voice sounds), your accent, your expressions, and your emotions. For example, you could have one grumpy character who sounds very posh and one very excitable character who has a high and squeaky voice.

STEP 2 Create one line for each character to "gossip", telling other guests about what has happened. It could be something like this: "Have you heard that a baby has been born in the place where the animals are kept? But not just any baby... *the* baby!" Or "That child was born among the stinky animals! I would never put anyone through that!"

STEP 3 Give each of your characters a line and add all the characters together to make into a performance sketch. Practise your sketch, and when you're ready, perform it to a wonderful audience!

DECK THE HALLS

Christmas is a wonderful time of celebration – and every celebration needs beautiful decorations!

Let's get creative!

It's time to create your own "Window Christmas Scene" to spread a little Christmas cheer to those who walk by!

In the evening, when it is dark and you have a light on in your house, the light will shine through, making shadows and outlines of your beautiful Christmas scene for everyone to enjoy!

YOU WILL NEED:

white paper
a pencil
scissors
sticky tack

STEP 1 On white paper, draw large silhouettes of houses with big windows, trees, shepherds, a baby in a manger, a big star... basically anything that you would like in your Christmas silhouette scene.

STEP 2 Cut out your silhouettes, including any holes for windows.

TOP TIP! If you have window holes in your houses, you could stick coloured tissue paper over the gaps to make it look like stained glass when the light shines through the window!

STEP 3 On the floor, arrange your paper shapes into a beautiful image of the first Christmas scene. Once you are happy with the formation of your silhouettes, use sticky tack to attach the paper shapes to your window.

Wow! That's cool!

TIME FOR A PARTY

Christmas is a time for parties and celebrations full of sparkle and fun! At great parties, you find people laughing with friends, dancing to "cheesy" music, and eating delicious nibbles!

People even gathered to celebrate at that very first Christmas Day. Imagine all those people crammed in with the animals, laughing, chatting, and celebrating together!

Let's get creative!

Why not organize a big celebration? Ask an adult to help you to plan a party where you can invite your friends, prepare nice food to share, and play fun festive music to get people dancing?

You could decorate a room with bright colourful decorations and celebrate the Christmas story in style!

In the space below, start to create a list of all the things you could do at your Christmas party! You could begin by creating a really fun party game like the pass-the-parcel game in this book ("A Story of Many Layers").

Christmas Party Planning

JOY TO THE WORLD

Carols have been sung for many years. At Christmas time, the sound of music and beautiful melodies often draws people together at carol services, concerts or around pianos!

Have you ever really read or listened to the words of carols? They tell the story of Christmas with beautiful poetic language. When you're singing the words, you can really imagine the scene!

Let's get creative!

Write and perform your very own Christmas carol!

STEP 1 Have a chat with an adult or a friend about what your favourite part of the Christmas story is.

STEP 2 Use the part of the story you have chosen as a starting point to write your own Christmas poem. Think about how you can use lots of descriptive words, like carols do, to help the people reading it to picture the scene. You could make your poem rhyme, or just describe the action or setting.

STEP 3 Once you have written your Christmas poem, create a melody to turn your poem into a carol to sing. You could use a melody you already know from an existing piece of music, or you could write your own tune completely from scratch!

STEP 4 Once you have practised singing the words, find an audience to listen as you perform your beautiful carol!

WOW!

What an epic journey we've had together, Creative Explorer!

Now that you have dived a little deeper into the story of Christmas, why not tell your friends about all the amazing things you have discovered?

You could even show them some of the cool things you have created along the way!

The great thing is you can use all these creative ideas again and again! They can be used all by yourself, in small groups, or in big groups.

The important thing is to never stop exploring, to never stop discovering new things, and of course to never stop having fun being creative!

Hope to see you again, Creative Explorer!

For more creative resources visit www.nimbuscollective.org

Look Out for

WOW! Jesus
ISBN 978 1 78128 425 4